THE TEN CHAPTERS OF LEADERSHIP

HOW TO BE A STRONG LEADER IN TEN EASY CHAPTERS

By

EJ Bones

THE TEN CHAPTERS OF LEADERSHIP

How To Be A Strong Leader

In Ten Easy Chapters

Published by EJ Bones

Copyright © 2014 by EJ Bones

Cover Art by EJ Bones

This book is protected under the copyright laws of the United States of America. Any reproduction or unauthorized use of the material or artwork herein is prohibited without the express written permission of the author.

First printing October 2014

First edition October 2014

INTRO

What exactly is leadership? And why is it so important? Let's start by defining the very thing that we are trying so hard to provide and fully understand:

LEADERSHIP: [lee-der-ship] A process of **social** influence in which one person can **enlist** the aid and support of others in the **accomplishment** of a common task.

When we read this definition there are a few words that seem to hold more significance than the others. Let's drill this down to three main ingredients.

Social: *Spent in or marked by friendly relations or companionship*

Being social is part of being a strong leader! Being a person who is friendly and thrives on building relationships (either with associates or customers for that matter) In order to provide the qualities of a strong leader we must be SOCIAL!

Enlist: *To engage the support or cooperation of*

A strong leader is able to engage a team! In other words LEAD them! This goes without saying. A leader is a person who has the ability to inspire people and help them to understand that what they provide to the team is as important as the overall mission.

Accomplishment: *Something completed successfully; an achievement*

What is the point, you ask??

The point is that we are working towards a goal and that goal equals SUCCESS! We want to accomplish something and we need an entire team to be able to do it!

That 'something' can be sales, customer service, solicitation, a grand opening, ANYTHING!

So a strong leader is a person who by way of social skills, is able to enlist a team, that will stop at nothing until they succeed and they will SMILE the entire time they are doing it!

Basically…..

So how are you going to do that?

Let's begin!

Chapter One

"ALLOW YOU TO INTRODUCE YOURSELF"

After years of being a retail store manager, district manager and director I have learned that the one thing you need to immediately do when you are a new leader of a team, is introduce yourself. And for that matter even if you are leading a team that you've been leading for a number of years and you finally are recognizing that you need to work on your leadership skills, you also need to introduce to that team who you are! As we have already determined, part of being a strong leader is being SOCIAL. That needs to begin with your team.

Think of yourself as walking into a social event filled with strangers. There are people all around you and they are all looking at you as you enter. They've never seen you before and they don't know why you're there and what you are doing. For that matter a certain percent of them don't really care. How are you going to handle it? What are you going to say? What are you going to do? Guess what? Those are the people that you are leading! Those are the ones that you need. Those are the ones that all of your goals, success and achievements rely on. You can't do it without them. So how are you going to make it happen? It's time to get busy!

Do you see yourself as the leader of the team? How do you think you do? Maybe you're not sure if you're a good leader or not? Maybe you feel that you MUST be because you've been in your position for a number of years and not everybody has quit! Maybe you actually believe that because people show up to work every day, they respect you as the leader? If you DO believe this you should wipe it from your mind immediately! The majority of people go to work to be paid, some of them enjoy it, and a few of them love it! But just because your team shows up for the job has nothing to do with YOU. Not yet, anyway!

Test yourself and see how strong of a leader you really are. Ask yourself a simple question and see how you do with the answer. We'll start with something easy:

Sit down at your desk, grab a pencil and paper. Now list on the paper every first name of every single person that works for you. How did you do? And no fair short changing your list! If you're a store manager you can't just list your assistant managers! You need to list every person that works in the building, including the maintenance man (if you have one). Was it easy? I hope it was easy! Because that's not really the test. That was the prep work for the test. This is the test:

Now write the LAST NAME of every single person in your building that works for you. This one's tougher, huh? And it's incredible how many managers are unable to do this. Maybe there's room to get closer and be more SOCIAL with your team?

If you struggle at just listing the first names, it should be extremely obvious to you that there is much to do. And if you flew through the entire assignment, challenge yourself to do more. If you know the first and last names of your entire team and your team is more than fifty people, that's GREAT! But that doesn't mean you pass the test. Push yourself! Do more! If the names are easy then take the assignment to the next level. List the towns that each person lives in next to their names! And if that's easy too, list their birthdays! How about eye color? You get the idea?

The goal of reading this book isn't to prove to yourself that you're already a strong leader. The goal is to make you think and develop you to be even stronger than you already are. Even if you're a great leader right now, push yourself! A true leader doesn't participate in a contest, win, get a trophy, bring it home and put it on the shelf. Then sit around and chew the fat about that time they won the race. A true leader is never done. They're always growing and they're always improving. You get the message? Be better!

Back to the room of strangers: Why would a team of strangers do what you say and feel good about it if they don't understand who you are? They, for a while may follow what you are directing just out of respect for your position and that they don't want to lose theirs. But that only lasts so long. If you want the team to believe in you, follow you, listen to what you have to say, and commit to it; they need to know who YOU are. Why else would they be interested? If they don't know you, I can guarantee they are just punching the clock and going home. And that's all you are accomplishing as their leader.

So who are you? What do you stand for? If you don't know the answer to these questions, then how the hell do you expect your team to know? Are you completely lost and overwhelmed by the idea of your introduction? Are you trying to figure out how to do this? It's okay if you are. We're going to get you through this.

I'll tell you first what NOT to do. Many years ago I met a person who wanted to get to know their team and they thought the best way to do it was to send each person a list of twenty questions. So they left a stack of the twenty questions in the break room and a poster of instruction for the team. The team reluctantly filled out the questionnaires and left the stack face down on the manager's desk. The majority of the team anticipated that there would be some sort of prize coming. They thought that perhaps this was the first step in a program. They were a bit irritated with the task but nonetheless had a bit of faith that there would be more to follow.

The manager looked at the completed stack of questionnaires for a minute or so. The manager shuffled them and read them and then left them in a stack on the corner of the desk. And that was where the stack stayed. It's probably still sitting there on the corner of that manager's desk! If that manager's still a manager that is! The point is this; the manager did nothing further. That was it. They were done.

The team was less than impressed and felt they had wasted their time on a foolish venture, which of course they had. The manager actually felt they had done a good thing and showed the team that they wanted to get to know them.

Talk about impersonalizing the efforts! Talk about dropping the ball. Talk about damaging a team that already doesn't know you, doesn't trust you and now probably never will! Okay so don't do anything like that!

Let's keep it simple. And remember that the idea is to introduce YOU. Part of being a leader is being social, we know this. Part of being social is getting to know the team and you will do that but you need to begin with an introduction of yourself!

The team wants to know who you are and what you're going to do. They want someone to follow. They want to trust you. But you're not going to get that right out of the gate. There are many ways you can begin to tell the team who you are and what you stand for. What kind of person are you? How are you going to help the team to be the best that they can be? Where is it all going to begin? Here's an example of what to do when you are introducing yourself to a team:

During your daily meetings, huddles, pep talks, whatever you call those moments when you bring your team together and tell them what's up for the day, week, month, year...whatever (If you're panicking as I'm discussing daily meetings and this is catching you by complete surprise...don't worry. Just remember to really focus when we get to Chapter Three) you have an opportunity to BEGIN introducing yourself.

Pretend it's your first day on the job. And you're right back in that room full of strangers that we talked about a couple of pages back. Your challenge is to introduce yourself to the crowd. How are you going to do it? Who are you? Tell them. And don't recite your resume! They already know you are the manager. You already have the job. A bit of background is okay but you're not at an interview. Personalize your introduction. Keep it mostly about you not your job. For example:

"Hello everybody! I want to introduce myself. My name is (insert name here). I've been with the company now for ten years and this is the third store I've worked in. I'm married and have been for thirty years now. My husband and I have five children. (Imagine oohs and laughter at that number) Yes...five! Their ages are...." You see where we are going with this right?

An introduction is about a person, not a job. The team wants to know who you are. You are not the first manager the team has ever had. They have some sort of sense for what a manager does. They want to know what YOU are going to bring to the table. What makes you different? What do you stand for? And why would they want to let you lead them?

You're not going to accomplish all of this with your introduction but you're going to consider the introduction your first step. It's okay to try and make your introduction fun for the team also!

Play a game! Call the game "Who knows who the new manager is?" Or call it "Get to know the manager." Tell your team three things about yourself and tell them that two are true and one is false. Whoever figures out which is what wins a prize! You will be amazed how much fun your team will have learning who you are as a person. Because once they do feel that they know you, they will want to join you in your quests. One time I did this with a new team and these were my examples:

1. In High School I played softball, basketball, swimming and cross country.
2. I have a body part from a cadaver inside of me.
3. I hate chocolate ice cream.

The person that won the game immediately received a prize! The prize wasn't a new car or anything extravagant. It was a simple brown paper bag filled with healthy snacks from the vending machine. The team had FUN with it! And the best part is that they were getting to know me as a person.

So what do you stand for? Now that you're introducing the person you have to certainly interject a tid-bit of 'what you stand for?' So what is it? What is your thing? What sets you apart from all other managers? Are you a manager that has the cleanest store in the world? Are you a manager that NEVER misses solicitation goals? Are you a manager that plants him or herself in the front of the store because you insist on shaking hands with every single customer? Are you the one that nails the truck unload every single time? Are you all about training? Add on sales? What? What do you stand for?

If the answer to this is nothing then you better figure it out and START standing for something! Give your team something to focus on more than anything else! They have a lot to do but I guarantee they want to be the best at something! There are so many different things that your team is responsible for every single day the second they show up for work. Your expectations as a leader is to do the best at every single goal and that goes without saying. But within all of those different things you do every single day, you need to be the best at one of them (at least). You need to have a clear vision of what you stand for and you need to lead your team to make sure that everybody in the company sees it! Your team wants this. They want to be known for being the team that leads the charge in something! And so do you! So what's your something?

Figure out what the something is and tell the team! And don't make the mistake of saying to yourself that you're going to lead in everything. This is not a book on *How to Overwhelm a Team*. Make it achievable.

I'll give you an example:

I am a manager that is all about customer service. I will not accept anything less than the best service that the company can provide for every single person that comes through that door. As that manager my introduction would sound like this:

"Hello everybody! I want to introduce myself. My name is EJ Bones. I've been a retail expert for nearly thirty years now and this is the second book I've written in regard to that. I'm married and have been for thirty years now. My husband and I have five children. (Imagine oohs and laughter at that number) Yes…five! They're all out of diapers and in fact live in their own homes now! (More than likely applause because this is a HUGE accomplishment).

My 'thing' if you will is customer service! Actually that's really all of ours' isn't it? (Chuckle) It is why we are here. It is everything that we do. The customer is the center of our universe actually because if we didn't have the customer our business wouldn't even exist! (Laughter) They are the reason we are here and they are the 'why' for everything that we do every single day!

I'm super excited to be here and I look forward to getting to know you all!"

Simple as that. The introduction is made. The team knows a bit about me and they understand that the number one focus we all will share is customer service. They will learn the hows, goals, challenges and rewards further down the road. Right now is the introduction phase. We don't need to solve the world's crisis during our introduction. We just need to say hello, this is who I am and this is what I stand for.

Your something will become their something. You will tell them, teach them, mentor them, train them, get to know them, LEAD THEM!

Chapter Two

BE A 'CONNECTER'

Okay, so you have introduced yourself and your focus to the team. What's next? You're not done. You just started! Now that you've opened the gates by talking to the team, you should want to make sure that the team realizes that the gate swings both ways.

Your next challenge is to be that person that every member of the team can be comfortable approaching. You are a leader and we already know that leaders are SOCIAL. Being social means that beyond the introduction you also need to be learning who your team is and what sort of strengths they bring to the table, which will help you and the entire team reach your goals. So how are you going to do that? How are you going to be that person that your team knows they can connect with? What does it take to be an approachable manager that is considered to be one of those people that is genuinely concerned, considerate and compassionate towards the team? Being a connector means being all of these things. Focus on the three C's. Let's study each 'C':

Concerned: How are you supposed to show your team that you are a concerned individual? What does that even mean? When you are a concerned person you are genuinely invested in the success of your team. You want them to do the best that they can do and you want them to enjoy doing it right?

A true leader always invests in some sort of performance management program for their associates. The associates should have a very good understanding of what they are expected to do and they should have help in doing it. Help can be in the form of many different things: training, mentorship programs, opportunities to learn other aspects of the position, option to apply for different positions, the chance to be involved in a project, and the list goes on and on and on. All of these things will show your team that you are concerned for them and their performance.

Considerate: What does it mean to be considerate? Being considerate means that you are the type of person that is careful to NOT hurt others. You respect them. You would never do anything to purposefully make them feel unworthy or useless.

Every member of every team has something to offer. There is something special that they bring to the table that WILL help you and the team to reach your goals. Your job as a leader is to figure out what those special talents are and put them to good use. Help the people to feel that they are contributing and that they are making a difference. Help them to feel good about what they are doing.

NEVER EVER humiliate people that work for you. That would be the opposite of considerate. That would be inconsiderate! You don't want to be that person. There's nothing to be proud of if you lead your team through intimidation and fear.

There's nothing worse than a boss that treats people with disrespect. Over my years in the retail world, I'm sorry to say I have worked for some real doozies! Those kinds of bosses that think nothing of tearing you down right in the center of the store for all of your fellow associates, colleagues, and customers to hear. Public humiliation is a horrible thing and something that a true leader would simply not do. There's no need to hurt people, yell at them, embarrass them. None of these things should be in your repertoire. The only good thing about a boss that treats people with disrespect is that they are teaching the team what NOT to do.

We all realize that part of our jobs as leaders, managers, directors, whatever, is to make sure that each person is contributing. And we all realize that there will be examples of associates that do not perform. As a leader you need to determine the difference between performance and behavior. If an associate has a performance issue they probably need more training, guidance, mentoring or direction. This is a positive thing requiring your expertise. The associate in all likelihood wants to do a good job but they don't know how to do that. They need your help so they can engage to the goals and bring their best to the team's efforts. People don't want to just watch from the sidelines when there's something exciting happening. They want to be a part of it.

On the contrary if the associate has a behavioral issue you need to find out what is going on and why. Even in this situation you should be considerate of their feelings and have a heart to heart conversation with them. If the associate is truly disengaged and has no intention of even trying to participate then you have no choice but to initiate counseling. (Next Book...How to Manage Associates Through Their Performance?) Through that process you will either save the associate or part as 'friends'. And even through that process there's no need to degrade or humiliate the associate. You as the leader are making sure that each associate has every opportunity to succeed.

Compassionate: What does it mean to be compassionate? A compassionate leader truly cares about the people that work for them. A compassionate leader is genuinely sympathizes for people. They are emotional towards other humans and see the other humans as being worth something. This is how we all should be. And as a leader it is even more imperative! You are the person that is to be engaging every member of the team to work towards the same goals. If you are the type of person that truly could care less about your team members, then you will not get very far as a leader.

We are all human right? Therefore there will be things that happen in all of our lives at one point or another and it will impact the entire team. These things can be tragic (death, divorce, illness) or happy occasions. (Marriage, birth of a child, vacations) As a leader you are the person that will manage these things effectively so as to not upset the apple cart. This is the easy part. But more importantly, as the leader you have an obligation to show the team and especially the individual that is 'dealing' with something, that you are compassionate.

Let me give you a quick opposite example of what I'm describing: Years ago I had a medical issue which required me to go out for an emergency surgery. I called my boss to tell him what was going on. He would be the one that would have to manage my absence seamlessly and effectively. He is a leader right?

Through the phone when I was struggling to explain to my boss what was happening, I could hear him breathing hard through his nose. Sort of like I would imagine an angry bull to sound just before it is preparing to charge straight toward me. And his massive body full of rage is about to throw my helpless body through the air like a ragdoll in the middle of an arena full of spectators.

I thought he would say he was concerned about my well-being. I thought he would have consideration for my feelings, because he most assuredly could hear the pain in my voice as I was being driven to an emergency room. He most assuredly could tell that I was not only in pain but quite upset about what was happening. I thought he would sympathize with me and my horrific situation. But none of this happened.

The one comment that my boss made to me over the phone on that day, in between his hot heavy breathing through his flared nostrils was, "How long are you going to be out for?" And guess what that did for me? Needless to say, I no longer work for that company.

Most people do not want to work for people that do not care about their well-being or the well-being of their family. Some people will quit a job before they continue to feel unimportant and unworthy. And if this is the atmosphere surrounding a team then most assuredly that team is not engaged to the goals. I can guarantee you that those people want nothing to do with the company, store, team or individual goals if they feel that their own boss could care less about them. Those people will do nothing beyond punching the clock and collecting a paycheck. And they will have no choice to do just that because they are not being led!

To be a strong leader you need to focus on the three C's. Show your team that you genuinely connect with them on many levels you are concerned, considerate and compassionate.

Chapter Three

THE MEANS TO COMMUNICATE

We all know what communication means. And when we think about communicating with a team we automatically picture ourselves standing at the head of the room and telling the team what's up, happening, coming, maybe how everybody did on something. And maybe this happens every single day or a couple of times a day. All of that is good, great and necessary. All of that should keep happening! But that is only a small portion of what communication is.

Communication is actually the SHARING or EXCHANGING of information. And sharing or exchanging information obviously requires that there is more than one individual involved. This mere definition implies that the sharing or exchanging of information is a two way street. The definition of communication isn't "A Lecture". Communication is when all involved parties are participating correct? Sort of like a back and forth exchange right? Sort of like a conversation right?

So if all parties involved are communicating effectively, how are they going to do that? What are the means of communication that you have available for the team? There are many different methods of sharing information. With large teams it is really necessary to have a few ways for people to communicate because not everybody wants to communicate the same way. Some people are shy and they prefer to communicate anonymously. Some people LOVE to be the center of attention and will stand up in the middle of an arena and start telling jokes! Make sure you have a few different means available for your team. Here are some methods and means for your associates to communicate with each other and with you:

- Face to Face
- Communication Notebook
- Huddles/Daily Meetings
- Bulletin Boards
- Email
- Telephone
- Suggestion Box
- Corporate Help Line Number
- Your Boss's Number

- One on One Regularly Scheduled Meetings
- All Day & Throughout the Day!
- Post It Notes
- Behind a Closed Door
- Over Lunch

And that's just a quick sampling of just some of the many ways that your team can communicate.

Your job as the leader is to make sure you have at least a few different ways for people to share information. As you are reading the above suggestion list you can't just say to yourself, "Well, we already have those in place. This goes without saying." Because to you and me it may certainly seem like it goes without saying…but maybe your associates don't really see it that way. Make sure you point it out to them. Or even invite them!

Make a point (during your daily huddles/meetings/etc) to say things like:

"For the next two hours I will be in my office with an open door. I am available if anybody needs to connect with me; so just come on in!"

"The bulletin board above the time clock is available for team communication. There is a stack of post it notes and pens on the table. Please feel free to use it for whatever you feel necessary. If you want to fill a shift…if you have an item on hold for a customer…if you want to say 'Happy Birthday'…anything!"

The important thing is to make sure you are providing them the MEANS to COMMUNICATE!

Chapter Four

FILL THE TOOL BOX

What tools? We need tools? Are we talking about hammers and screwdrivers?? Well, maybe. But not necessarily.

What is a tool? When I think of a tool I think of a gadget that I use with my hands to repair, build, or tear something up. But by mere definition a tool is *something regarded as necessary to the carrying out of one's occupation or profession.* Tools can therefore be about anything! Tools can be a host of different things that each associate requires in order to get their jobs done effectively and efficiently.

Tools can be gadgets or actual 'things':

- Pens
- Paper
- Change at the register
- Sales flyers
- Bags
- Stapler

Tools can also be:

- Training
- Information
- Service Skills
- TIME!!! (that's a GOOD one)

Everything and anything that is used in order to complete the task at hand is considered to be a tool. As the leader, it is your job to make sure your team has the tools they need to do their jobs. The easy part is the gadgets! This is nothing more than ordering supplies and ensuring that they are completely stocked and available at all times. Piece of cake! You can even post a "We Need This" list at the entrance to a supply closet to make sure you or your administrative assistant never overlooks needed tools.

The rest of the 'stuff' is the more challenging part of keeping the tool box full. And why is this so important? Why do we need anything beyond the gadgets?

Think of it this way: One of the number one reasons people quit their job is because they feel the work load is unrealistic. People will quit if they feel they are unable to complete the tasks at hand. People will quit if they are too frustrated. Nobody likes to be under complete duress every single day. Nobody likes to feel like they are failing every single day. And if people are being challenged to complete tasks or do the job but they don't have the means to be able to do just that...they will WALK!

So give them the means. What do they need? Forget about the gadgets for a second. Do you truly think an associate will quit their job because they can't find a pen? Well maybe...but not likely. It's beyond the gadgets!

One of the BEST ways to figure out what your associates need in the tool box is to ask them! Come right out and pick a topic that they are required to focus on and ask them how it's going! It's that easy. Example:

Your associates are all required to solicit customers to sign up for the company credit/charge card. Yet they consistently fail and fumble in achieving the goals.

At your next daily meeting you say: "Talk to me about soliciting. How does it work? Are you comfortable with it? Why not? What is the hurdle?"

You may hear from your associates that they don't know what to say. The customers ask questions that they don't have the answers to. They don't know how to input the information for the customer to sign up so they avoid the entire topic. You may hear that you have a training issue! You may hear that you need to schedule some mentoring shifts with new people and the veteran staff members.

The point is that you as the leader are obligated to FILL THE TOOL BOX! And you need to talk with your team to find out what goes in the box!

Chapter Five

GOALS, GOALS, GOALS!

What are we doing? What are the expectations? What are we working towards? How are we going to do it? Where do I fit in? How does my performance impact the team? What direction are we going in? What is the point, already???

These are all excellent questions that probably most of your associates will want the answers to. And if you think of all the goals that you have as the manager of a business and team, there are probably hundreds of them! So how are you going to communicate goals to a team and help them to understand that their performance is important and pertinent to the results?

Well, we already know that this book is not *How to Overwhelm a Team.* So you, as the leader, will want to communicate achievable team goals that clearly relate to the associates performance. There should always be more than one goal but probably no more than three. Ideally you want the three goals to work towards the overall store/organization goals. Focus on the three top aspects of running your business and develop your goals for the team/associates from there. For example:

1. PEOPLE: One of the three goals should be focused on the people that make your team. A leader knows that all results are achieved through the enlistment of the team. The team

needs to be included in the goals. What do you want to stand for when it comes to the associates that work for you? And how are you going to measure it? Examples of people goals:

- Safety First! Go an entire year without a work place accident.
- Associate of the Month! Make a goal to award one associate per month with top honors.
- Perfect Attendance Award! Who is the best in the store and what do they win for NEVER calling out?

2. CUSTOMER: Your second goal should be focused on the customer. Without the customer we all cease to exist. They are the most important reason for all of our

performance and can never be overlooked! (Suggested reading: ***EXCELLENT CUSTOMER SERVICE – How to Build a Customer Service Culture in a Retail Environment*** by EJ Bones) Examples of customer goals:

- Credit for Customers! Create a goal that is OVER the requirement for credit solicitation. Draw a giant thermometer in the break-room and have associates take turns coloring in the daily achievements!

- Survey Says! Does the company you work for have a customer survey program? Challenge your associates to obtain record numbers of surveys. Everybody knows that the more surveys you obtain the stronger your yearly results are. If you typically get ten customer surveys per week…shoot for twenty, or thirty or how about ten a day?!

- Customer Connections! Initiate a program that requires an in-house one-on-one customer survey to be obtained. Every Wednesday ask customers THREE targeted questions. Read the results during your daily meetings. React to the customer feedback.

3. PRODUCTIVITY: It all comes down to the results right? One of the goals needs to be about the numbers! What are we working towards and what are the results of those

efforts to the bottom line? Examples of productivity goals:

- TACK IT ON! Challenge the team to suggestive sell a counter-top item every week. Try making it fun! Chose items that are TOUGH sellers. Chose items that you have a lot of and you want to get rid of! Chose items that are seasonal because you only have so long to make these items move! How many can they sell?

- NEAT FREAKS! We all know that presentation is everything. When the goods are neat, orderly, sized, and pretty they will sell better. Pick a section of the store that needs special attention in order to sell the goods and track the results. Ensure that each day a person is assigned to be the 'neat freak'.

- TOP with the TRUCK! Develop a goal that involves the truck unload process. Does your company give you a set number of hours for unload? BEAT IT! Then put the remaining hours into "fun tasks" such as painting the break room, or rearranging a department that needs it, anything at all that your team wants to do!

The main focus here is to be clear. Let your team know what they should be focusing on. Share the progress and results with them on a daily basis! Don't just put up a poster and expect that they will produce results from that. Your associates should be so well versed with the goals that if your boss were to walk through the door and ask them all to recite the goals; each associate would answer exactly the same way!   If that seems unachievable for YOU...then you as the LEADER knows what your individual goal should be! Your goal should be to develop the team goals!

Chapter Six

RECOGNITION PROGRAM

This is my favorite part! This is the part that feels like a party! This is the part that everybody loves! This is the part that often times is what keeps your associates engaged!

EVERYBODY wants to be appreciated! If you were to walk down a city block and literally ask every single person you passed if they like feeling appreciated in the work place, I can guarantee you they would ALL say YES! Think about it! Who doesn't want to feel good about what they do? Are there any people out there that don't want to be appreciated? Are there any people out there that want to feel like they're not wanted, like they're failing, like they're going to get in trouble? Probably not! Human nature is that we LIKE to feel good! Human nature is to be happy. It's not to be miserable. We like feeling good about ourselves! And we are worth it! Your associates are worth it!

So if appreciation is that important…you as the leader need to do it! So what are you doing? What sort of recognition programs do you have in place? And when I say have in place, I mean actually USING! You can't get credit for reciting recognition programs that your company suggests or directs if you as the leader aren't engaged to using them. Recognition needs to be structured and it without fail needs to be consistent! Without consistency your program means nothing. And you as the leader will mean nothing to your team if you do not show them how much you appreciate them!

Lots of pressure on this one. So what should you do? What sort of programs will work? Should there be more than one? Think of it like a layer cake. Your recognition program should have at least three layers of cake; otherwise it's really just a morsel. When I eat a piece of cake I want a nice big piece of cake! Two layers just won't do it. A cake rounds out the entire mean quite nicely doesn't it? Let's study our cake:

First Layer: Daily recognition.

Throughout your day as the leader you should be seeing numerous opportunities to recognize people. And recognition doesn't always have to mean a prize or a ceremony. A huge part of recognition is noticing the work that people are doing, and telling them that they are doing it well. A thank you goes a very long way and often times is exactly what the associate needs to continue improving their performance. Make a point as the leader to always be watching, listening, coaching and recognizing your team's efforts!

Every day there should be a meeting of some sort with the team. We've mentioned it a number of times already and this is a valuable step to making sure that not only are you giving your team means to communicate but you are also scheduling an opportunity to recognize some of your stars. A daily meeting should always recognize the previous day's results! This will keep your goals alive and will show your team that you as the leader are consistently following through with communication, goals and recognition. The daily meeting MUST HAPPEN!

Daily recognition can be for the entire team or individuals in any of these areas:

- Sales
- Solicitation
- Customer Comments
- Manager's Pick (best performance of the team from the previous day)
- Remember the previous chapter on goals? GOALS. Recognize the team's results as they pertain to the goals you have developed.

You might want to create a "Daily Meeting Form" to ensure that each member of management is following the same structure when they host the daily meetings. Consistency!

Second Layer: Weekly recognition. (You see where we're going with this right?)

Pick a day of the week and focus on the previous week's results. (Probably Monday) During that day's meeting not only would you recognize results from the previous day but from the previous week as well.

In the second layer of recognition I strongly encourage you to present some sort of award to the people that you are recognizing. And the award doesn't have to be anything big but just the fact that you are presenting it will be BIG to your team.

Examples:

- The leader of the *"Tack it ON"* goal receives a small box of neon colored tacks!!

- The associate that solicited the highest number of customer surveys receives a new pen with the company logo on it!
- The associate that presented a safety concern to management receives a box of bandages!

If any of these suggestions are too big or expensive because you are a very small business, then present your associate with a hand-made thank you card!

Anything at all works! The important thing is that you are noticing and you are recognizing.

Third Layer: I'll bet you can guess…..MONTHLY recognition!

This layer of the cake requires a bit more attention and announcement. This is when you get to put up posters in the break room. And you present the news during the first three daily meetings of each month to make sure that everybody hears the news.

Examples of monthly recognition:

- People's Choice – have associates nominate a person as associate of the month.
- TOP Solicitor – The best of the best gets a monthly award for signing more customers up for the charge card than any other associate! The prize can be THREE EXTRA FIFTEEN MINUTE BREAKS!
- Manager's Choice – You get to pick it! And it can be for anything at all. Maybe you have an associate that cleaned the

back room and it's the most beautiful back room you have ever seen! Maybe you have an associate that traveled to a neighboring store to help when a member of their team had taken ill. Maybe you have an associate that hand delivered an item to a customer that's elderly. YOU PICK IT! And the prize can be a brown bag lunch with the manager. Thirty minutes…you each bring your own lunch…and you get to know that associate.

And the **ICING ON THE CAKE**…YEARLY RECOGNITION!

How did the team do? Were all the goals met? How are you going to celebrate all of the hard work and efforts for the entire team? Your yearly recognition should be delivered during some sort of event. This is the big one! This is the big deal! This is the moment when you tie all of the efforts in with all of the goals and you announce to the entire team how much you appreciate all of their hard work!

So how are you going to do that? The best course of action is to plan ahead. Put some effort into it. Show the team that you are serious when you show appreciation. You may want to put together a small team as a YEARLY EVENT COMMITTEE. Perhaps you will need to rent a space for your event? Or maybe the entire team goes bowling? You host a barbeque? You go to a state park or beach? Whatever venue you or your committee decides on you may need to do some fund raising. Throughout the year you may want to hold small bake sales or lunches and save the money for the yearly event. Plan ahead!

During your event you will probably need an entire hour for presentations and awards of recognition. And there should be some BIG DEAL awards handed out! These awards should focus on your goals (of course).

Examples:

- THE PEOPLE GOAL WINNER receives a trophy with a person on top and a little brass plate that states what they achieved!
- THE CUSTOMER GOAL WINNER receives a NICE pen!

- THE PRODUCTIVITY GOAL WINNER receives gift card to the store you all work at…because it's all about the sales and numbers right?
- ASSOCIATE OF THE YEAR receives the best parking space in the lot for the entire year!
- MANAGER'S PICK gets an entire week off with pay!

And maybe every single person that works for you receives a certificate of appreciation that is personalized and focused on that one great thing that they bring to the table every single day they work!

Whatever you come up with should feel like the grand finale of recognition! Your yearly event needs to be a BIG DEAL! Because it is a big deal. Your team is engaged and they are trying to do a good job. They should know that you see it. You should see it!

Make it big! Make it special! Focus on the goals! Show how much you appreciate your team! Every day, week, month & year!

Chapter Seven

FOLLOW UP

One of many signs of a strong leader is a person who follows up. Follow up is a part of nearly everything we do as leaders. Nearly every chapter in this book can connect to the importance of follow up. We talked about recognition: What good does it do to put together a recognition program if you're not going to identify the winners or present awards? We talked about communication: What good does it do to have a conversation with people or ask them for feedback if you're not going to follow up with them after the fact? Or maybe even get them answers they need to do a better job? We talked about goals. What good does it do to develop goals for a team if you never let them know how they are doing? All of these things require that you follow up with your team. For the purposes of our discussion we will use an example involving GOALS.

Why is this so important? What exactly does follow up even mean? As we explore the importance of follow up, think of it like this - Follow up is the B.E.S.T. thing you can do for your entire team! B E S T… and that is exactly how you can remember it:

1. **B** is for BEGIN – this is when it all begins! This is the step that stands for the initiation of the goal. This is like the birthday for the goal. What are you and your team focusing on? This is where the creative juices take over and you and your team decide what you WILL be

the best at! And this step should include people that are on your team. It shouldn't always and only come from you. A leader as we know involves and inspires others. This is a group effort.

2. **E** - is for EXPLAIN – You need to tell everybody what the plan is! Remember we want your boss or your boss's boss to come into your four walls, ask each person what the goals are, and get the same answer.

   Explaining clearly and precisely is a MUST when it comes to follow up!

   Explain doesn't just happen one time either! Part of explaining is continuous. This is not a one-time event. As a leader it is your job to keep the focus on goals. Keep reminding people what you are all working toward.

Keep recognizing the amazing efforts that you will see! Explaining happens over quite a period of time; such as the year! Keep the story alive!

3. **S -** is for SIMPLIFY. How do we simplify? Simplifying things means that we are making them easier. As a team begins to work on a common goal there will in all likelihood be things that come up and present challenges along the way. You as the leader will be reacting to these challenges, suggestions, feedback, etc. This is the meat of the matter when it comes to follow up. It may involve additional training, acquiring tools, restructuring the team a bit, hiring additional people with specific skills, anything at all. You and your team will continue to grow and

develop yourselves to be the true experts as you progress on completing and BEATING your goals!

4. **T** - is for TOTAL! This is when we measure the results! Did it work? How did you do? Your TOTAL should also be something that happens a number of times as your team progresses. Daily, weekly, monthly, yearly! Goals are measureable. Once the goal is set and your team has begun to dig in, you will want to ensure that the results are constantly being measures, studied, focused on. The TOTAL can be put on the bulletin board, updated daily, spoken about during daily meetings, everything! Make sure to keep the numbers out there!

And there you have it:

Begin   **E**xplain   **S**implify   **T**otal

Equals…Follow UP!

Chapter Eight

THE UNTOUCHABLES

As a leader you have a lot to do! Your plate is completely full and you are juggling many things in the air at the same time. So in this chapter, I'm going to give you a break and give you something to NOT DO!

There are some things which in the middle of everything else that you do…no matter what you do, as the leader of a team, you cannot and MUST NOT EVER DO. There are some things that you just should not ever mess with! These things are considered to be the "Untouchables"!

They are the things that will cause your associates to be thrust into a full blown rage to the point that they may even quit their jobs if you do mess with the "Untouchables". The "Untouchables" are like a living breathing thing. You need to feed them. Take care of them. Appreciate them. But never ever upset them. They exist and are necessary and are definitely things that you need to manage and be effective with. Don't look directly at them. They can never be taken away, or upset, or overlooked. There is a very delicate balance between associates and the "Untouchables". The "Untouchables" should be protected at all times.

Of course I'm exaggerating slightly for effect. But the truth of the matter is that there are some things that as a leader you just know cannot be messed with. They are the things that are SO important to your associates that you can seriously lose very good people over if you fail to manage these things correctly.

So what are the "Untouchables" you ask?

Three things:

1. **BREAKS**
2. **SCHEDULE**
3. **PAY**

Many years ago I watched the complete breakdown of an entire team because one of the "Untouchables" was overlooked. I was brand new to the company that I worked for. I had been hired as a part-time cashier. And on one particular day I was quietly sitting in the break room waiting to punch in for my four hour shift when all of the sudden all hell broke loose!

A veteran staff member came storming into the break room from the selling floor, snatched the telephone off the wall and directly called the Regional Manager for that particular store. The veteran staff member then proceeded to leave a '911' voice mail for the Regional Manager.

"Calling all Regional Managers! We have an emergency at the Main Street store! The paychecks have not arrived and according to the office manager, payroll was never approved this week. Mayday! Mayday! Mayday!"

And with that he slammed down the receiver and stormed back out to the selling floor. Within moments there was an entire parade of irate associates marching into the office by way of the break room. And long story short, the company sent a District Administrative Assistant to the store with a check book to take care of the entire team's paychecks before there was a mass exodus! It was quite a scene! One of which I was a silent partner in. I mean I wanted my paycheck too. I was a young mouth of only two tiny children at the time and I had ventured into the world of retail to earn money for my groceries and baby formula. (those were the days)

And then there are the BREAKS! Breaks cannot ever be overlooked or you will not only have a riot on your hands but you will potentially have corporate breathing down your neck and the State knocking on your door! It's a LAW! And people deserve rest without interruption!

Hell, as a strong leader that shows compassion and concern and connects with your team…you should be offering extra breaks for jobs well done, or if an associate is feeling under the weather. For years I have been one of those managers that focuses so much on breaks for the team that I often will think of any and all reasons to have snack food in the break room!

"Today's Pancakes for LUNCH day! Help yourself!"

"Time for a Chili Cook Off!"

"Take an Extra FIVE Day!" All associates are encouraged to grab an extra five minute break today and enjoy the delicious chip and dip special on the break room table! (Throw some carrot sticks in there for good measure)

And that brings us to SCHEDULES. This one should be easy right? People give us their availability and we have programs or very clever people plug in availability to match business needs and out pops a perfect schedule that everybody loves, right?

WRONG…

I remember years ago, I was a brand new assistant manager for a retail store that had a team of approximately one-hundred seventy-five people. My first week at this new store tragedy struck. The store manager (my boss) lost his mother-in-law and had to travel to the other side of the world for a week long mourning ceremony, one of the other assistant managers was already on vacation and was on a tropical island somewhere in the middle of the Atlantic Ocean, and the other assistant manager's house burned down! That left me a two Area Supervisors to run the store. But more importantly it left me and a brand new administrative assistant to put together a schedule for the huge team (of which I knew nobody) and none of their availabilities were up to date in the schedule system. Quite a challenge!

So I did what we leaders do. I called for help, solicited help from neighboring store, called in department heads from the selling floor, and managed to put together a schedule and got it posted! I was so proud!

But guess what? I posted the schedule late! The schedule was supposed to post at eight o'clock

Saturday morning and I didn't get it posted until two o'clock that afternoon.

So guess what happened? Somebody called corporate head-quarters and complained. And guess who got in trouble...first week on the job? Yep. Unreasonable on the part of the person that made that call? Probably. That's not the point. The point is just the importance of the...

"Untouchables"

(Don't mess with them!)

Chapter Nine

BE A PART OF SOMETHING BIGGER THAN YOU ARE!

You've done a great job at leading the team! Things are heading in the right direction! Your associates are engaging to the goals and they are working hard to deliver strong results!

What else can you do?

You're not done! You are never done! Part of being a leader is always striving to improve! Always inspiring others to improve! Now let's focus on taking it to the next level! What else can you accomplish? What else is there for the team to feel good about? Take a step beyond the walls and look to become even bigger and better than what you currently are as a team! It's time to shoot for the stars!

What am I talking about? Let me give you a couple of examples:

There's a certain potato chip company that recently (maybe currently) had a contest to come up with a new potato chip flavor. They advertised it nationally, they put it all over the internet, they splashed the rules on the sides of all of the bags of potato chips they made. And people responded! People went on line through their own social web pages and entered the contest. And the winner of the contest wins something like a million dollars! Do you know what I'm speaking of? Did you enter?

I entered! I sent in ideas for Sugar & Spice Chips, PB & J Chips, Chocolate Chips….anything I could think of. For one I wanted to win the money! But I also wanted to be a part of all the excitement! I wanted to sign onto the web-page of the potato-chip company and watch and read to see who won the contest. AND…I wanted to taste all of the entries! I wanted to be a part of something bigger than what I was. It was exciting!

(I didn't win by the way)

Another example: How many of you poured a bucket of cold ice water over your head?

You get the point?

As a leader, you have the opportunity to take your team to the next level! Encourage them to be a part of something bigger than they already are! You never know how amazing your team can be unless you are always thinking, creating and encouraging growth and development!

So what are you going to do?

What can you accomplish together?

Have you ever heard of that company in Seattle that throws fish across the market? Perfect example!

Start with what you know. Begin with that one thing that you want to be the best at. Build it from there!

(Think)

Chapter Ten

WALK IT & TALK IT

You've all heard that expression: "Walk the walk and talk the talk." What does it mean?

Basically it means two things. One is that you (or somebody) talks the talk. They say all of the right things. They know what needs to happen and they tell you all of those things and they are correct!

And then there's walk the walk. And that means that the person does all of the right things. They are the ones that take the action and make sure that the job gets done.

Put both of these things together and you have a strong leader. *Walking the Walk and Talking the Talk* should be your golden rule! You can't be one of those people that says all of the right things but does all the wrong. And you can't be one of those people that says everything wrong but takes action on the tasks correctly. Those are the kind of people that leave injured parties along the way. Those aren't the kind of people that show strength and commitment with not only what they say but what they do. Therefore: Don't just say it....DO IT!

It doesn't count if you say it but you never hold your own actions to the same level of your associates. You are the leader. You are the one they will look to, listen to, follow and respect. If you are getting that much attention with all eyes on you, then perhaps you should be leading the team with the best example of what you ask of them! Show your team how to get done what you say will get done.

Encourage them.

Lead them.

They will follow you.

They will respect you.

You will succeed!

IN CLOSING...

Congratulations! You have completed the entire book and you have learned about everything you need to be a strong LEADER!

- *THE INTRODUCTION*
- *BE A CONNECTER*
- *THE MEANS TO COMMUNICATE*
- *THE TOOL BOX*
- *FOLLOW UP*
- *GOALS, GOALS, GOALS*
- *RECOGNITION PROGRAM*
- *PROTECTION FOR THE "UNTOUCHABLES"*
- *BE A PART OF SOMETHING BIGGER THAN YOU ARE*
- *WALK IT & TALK IT*

I know you and your teams will be completely amazing and would love to hear your stories of success!

EJBones@outlook.com

Or

EJ Bones@EJBones1 (via Twitter)

Wishing you the greatest success!

www.ingramcontent.com/pod-product-compliance
Lightning Source LLC
Chambersburg PA
CBHW071747170526
45167CB00003B/970